Colorful Quilts for Kids

by Christiane Meunier

CHITRA PUBLICATIONS

Your Best Value in Quilting

Chitra Publications
2 Public Avenue
Montrose, Pennsylvania 18801-1220

First printing: 1999
Library of Congress Cataloging-in-Publication Data

Meunier, Christiane, 1952-
    Colorful quilts for kids / by Christiane Meunier.
      p.cm.
    ISBN 1-885588-29-1
      1. Quilting-Patterns. 2. Children's quilts. I. Title

    TT835 .M4854 1999
    746.46'041--dc21
                                        99-050259

Edited by: Debbie Hearn
Design & Illustration: Diane Albeck-Grick
Cover Photography: Guy Cali Associates, Clarks Summit, PA
Inside Quilt Photography: VanZandbergen Photography, Brackney, PA
and Carina Woolrich, San Diego, CA

Our Mission Statement:

*We publish quality quilting magazines and books
that recognize, promote and inspire self-expression.
We are dedicated to serving our customers
with respect, kindness and efficiency.*

Children brighten up our lives. I think it's fun to return some of that brightness by stitching colorful quilts for them. That's why I've gathered a dozen lively quilts to pattern in this book. And here's a secret—they're not just for kids! These wall-size and lap-size quilts are sure to appeal to all ages.

Making the quilts is like child's play thanks to the easy, no-template construction methods used for most of them. That leaves you free to focus on fabrics and color to give each quilt a one-of-a-kind look. It's my favorite part of making quilts! For example, "Baby's First Nine Patch" gets dynamic movement from using a green stripe for the setting triangles and varying the colors of the plain squares placed between scrappy Nine Patch blocks. "Four-Patch Confetti" is as traditional and easy as piecing gets. Its pizzazz comes from bright calico fabrics. Crazy pieced fish swim on a marine blue background in "Gone Fishin'," which also features a no-fuss pieced-look border.

Kids love gifts that have that personal, "just-for-you" feeling. Celebrate a child's special interest by using novelty fabrics. "Farmer in Training" is a simple Log Cabin that becomes more intriguing because the center squares include a tractor motif cut from a print fabric. Or make a truly individual expression when you transfer photos to fabric for a quilt. That's how "Picture Windows," a nine-block Attic Windows quilt, and "Little Stars" each offer a peek into precious lives. The birth of a grandchild is an occasion that yearns to be commemorated with a special quilt. My friend, Sharyn Craig, expressed her joy by making "Alphabet Quilt." In it, she combined pieced blocks in primary colors with a fusible appliqué alphabet.

I've noticed that simple shapes repeated in various colors attract kids. Square-in-a-square blocks make up "Tic-Tac-Toe," pieced in deep jewel tones. "Snail's Trail" provides a fascinating tessellating pattern to gaze at, while hourglass units in the center of "Wading Pool" are repeated in the border.

Kids are full of surprises and your quilts can be, too. The rectangular strips of "Climbing the Rail Fence" create a whimsically random pattern when you vary the color placement. Doing this results in a block that is less static than one pieced in the usual color sequence. "Pinwheel" uses a single shape in a tessellating pattern. This one is lots of fun to assemble on a design wall by auditioning fabric pieces for best placement. Ask a child to help you. Children have a gift for knowing what looks just right. Working together is a bonus that will make the quilt even more special.

I hope you enjoy stitching these quilts. Any of them would make a special heartfelt gift for a favorite child. Do you have one in mind?

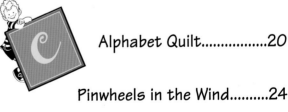

Contents

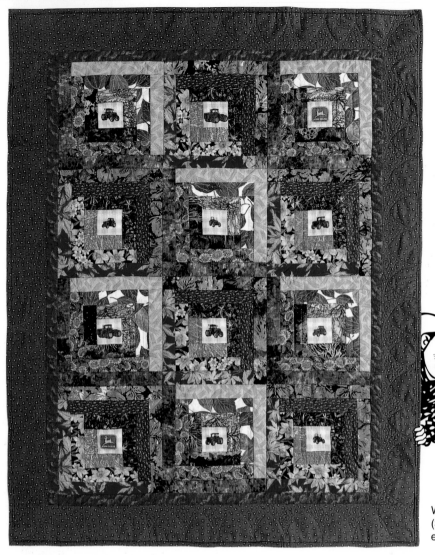

Farmer in Training

Tractor power for the earth-tender of tomorrow!

What young man doesn't like tractors? **"Farmer in Training"** (37 1/2" x 47 1/2") is sure to make some little guy happy. I used earth colors to piece this down-on-the-farm quilt.

QUILT SIZE: 37 1/2" x 47 1/2"
BLOCK SIZE: 9 3/4" square

MATERIALS

Yardage is estimated for 44" fabric.
• 12 tractor fabric motifs to be centered in a 2 3/4" square
• 1/8 yard each of 6 gold prints
• 1/8 yard each of 6 dark prints, (2 green prints, 3 blue prints and a brown print)
• 1/4 yard rust print, for the inner border
• 1 yard blue print, for the border and binding
• 1 1/2 yards backing fabric
• 42" x 52" piece of batting

CUTTING

Dimensions include a 1/4" seam allowance.
• Cut 12: 2 3/4" squares, tractor print, centering a motif in each square
• Cut 6: 1 3/4" x 2 3/4" strips, first gold print
• Cut 6: 1 3/4" x 4" strips, first gold print

• Cut 6: 1 3/4" x 5 1/4" strips, second gold print
• Cut 6: 1 3/4" x 6 1/2" strips, second gold print
• Cut 6: 1 3/4" x 7 3/4" strips, third gold print
• Cut 6: 1 3/4" x 9" strips, third gold print
• Cut 6: 1 3/4" x 2 3/4" strips, fourth gold print
• Cut 6: 1 3/4" x 4" strips, fourth gold print
• Cut 6: 1 3/4" x 5 1/4" strips, fifth gold print
• Cut 6: 1 3/4" x 6 1/2" strips, fifth gold print
• Cut 6: 1 3/4" x 7 3/4" strips, sixth gold print
• Cut 6: 1 3/4" x 9" strips, sixth gold print
• Cut 6: 1 3/4" x 4" strips, first green print
• Cut 6: 1 3/4" x 5 1/4" strips, first green print

• Cut 6: 1 3/4" x 6 1/2" strips, first blue print
• Cut 6: 1 3/4" x 7 3/4" strips, first blue print
• Cut 6: 1 3/4" x 9" strips, brown print
• Cut 6: 1 3/4" x 10 1/4" strips, brown print
• Cut 6: 1 3/4" x 4" strips, second green print
• Cut 6: 1 3/4" x 5 1/4" strips, second green print
• Cut 6: 1 3/4" x 6 1/2" strips, second blue print
• Cut 6: 1 3/4" x 7 3/4" strips, second blue print
• Cut 6: 1 3/4" x 9" strips, third blue print
• Cut 6: 1 3/4" x 10 1/4" strips, third blue print
• Cut 4: 1 1/2" x 44" strips, rust print, for the inner border
• Cut 4: 3 1/2" x 44" strips, blue print, for the outer border

- Cut 5: 2 1/2" x 44" strips, blue print, for the binding

DIRECTIONS

- Stitch a 1 3/4" x 2 3/4" first gold print strip to the right side of a 2 3/4" tractor square, as shown.

- Stitch a 1 3/4" x 4" first gold print strip to the top of the unit, as shown.

- Stitch a 1 3/4" x 4" first green print strip to the left side of the unit.

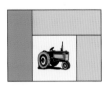

- Stitch a 1 3/4" x 5 1/4" first green print strip to the bottom of the unit.

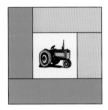

- Referring to the quilt photo for color placement as necessary, continue adding strips to the unit, working in a counter-clockwise direction. Stitch the second and third gold print strips to the right and top. Stitch the first blue print strips and the brown print strips to the left and bottom to complete the block. Make 6.

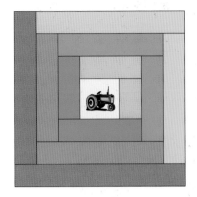

- Stitch a 1 3/4" x 2 3/4" fourth gold print strip to the left side of a 2 3/4" tractor square, as shown.

- Stitch a 1 3/4" x 4" fourth gold print strip to the bottom of the unit.

- Stitch a 1 3/4" x 4" second green print strip to the right side of the unit.

- Stitch a 1 3/4" x 5 1/4" second green print strip to the top of the unit.

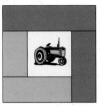

- Referring to the quilt photo for color placement as necessary, continue adding strips to the unit, this time stitching the 5th and 6th gold print strips to the left and bottom and the remaining blue print strips to the right and top to complete the block. Make 6.
- Referring to the quilt photo for color placement, lay out the blocks in 4 rows of 3. Stitch the blocks into rows and join the rows.
- Measure the length of the quilt. Trim 2 of the 1 1/2" x 44" rust print strips to that measurement. Stitch them to the sides of the quilt.
- Measure the width of the quilt, including the borders. Trim the remaining 1 1/2" x 44" rust print strips to that measurement and stitch them to the top and bottom of the quilt.
- In the same manner, trim 2 of the 3 1/2" x 44" blue print strips to fit the quilt's length and stitch them to the sides of the quilt.
- Trim the remaining 3 1/2" x 44" blue print strips to fit the quilt's width and stitch them to the top and bottom of the quilt.
- Finish the quilt as described in the *General Directions*, using the 2 1/2" x 44" blue print strips for the binding.

Gone Fishin'

How many fish
do you wish?
Stitch a
half dozen
to use in this
lively quilt!

Have you ever noticed how fascinated children are with an aquarium teaming with tropical fish? Here's a quick quilt that shows off 6 bright creatures of the sea. **"Gone Fishin'"** (41" x 31") is easy to make with foundation piecing.

QUILT SIZE: 41" x 31"
BLOCK SIZE: 8 1/2" square

MATERIALS
Yardage is estimated for 44" fabric.
- Assorted bright stripes and dots in red, yellow and green, totaling at least 1/2 yard
- Assorted scraps of hand-dyed orange, fuchsia and yellow, totaling at least 1/2 yard
- 1/2 yard red with blue dots, for the binding
- 1 yard mottled blue
- 1/8 yard yellow wavy stripe
- 1/8 yard red wavy stripe
- 1/8 yard blue with red dots
- 1/8 yard wide stripe
- 1 1/4 yards backing fabric
- 35" x 45" piece of batting
- Paper for the foundations

CUTTING
Dimensions include a 1/4" seam allowance. Fabric for foundation piecing will be cut as you stitch the blocks. Each piece must be at least 1/2" larger on all sides than the section it will cover. Refer to the General Directions as needed.
- Cut 4: 2" x 9" strips, mottled blue
- Cut 1: 2" x 29" strip, mottled blue
- Cut 2: 2" x 25" strips, mottled blue
- Cut 2: 4" x 25" strips, mottled blue
- Cut 2: 2" x 35" strips, mottled blue
- Cut 2: 4" x 35" strips, mottled blue
- Cut 6: 5 1/2" squares, mottled blue, then cut them in half diagonally to yield 12 triangles
- Cut 1: 1 1/2" x 25" strip, blue with red dots
- Cut 1: 1 1/2" x 35" strip, blue with red dots
- Cut 4: 2 1/2" x 44" strips, red with blue dots, for the binding
- Cut 1: 1 1/2" x 25" strip, wide stripe
- Cut 1: 1 1/2" x 35" strip, wide stripe

DIRECTIONS
- Trace the full-size patterns (on pages 30 and 31) on the foundation paper, transferring all lines and numbers and leaving a 1" space between foundations. Make 6 of Block A and 6 of Block B. Cut each one

out 1/2" beyond the broken line.
- Follow the foundation piecing instructions in the *General Directions* to piece the blocks.
For the Block A's:
- Use the following fabrics in these positions:
  - 1 - yellow
  - 2 - green stripe
  - 3 - fuchsia
  - 4 - assorted stripes
  - 5 - green print
  - 6 - red print
  - 7 - wide print stripe
  - 8 - orange
  - 9 - red print
For the Block B's:
- Use the following fabrics in these positions for 2 of the blocks:
  - 1 - mottled blue
  - 2 - red wavy stripe
- Use the following fabrics in these positions for the remaining 4 blocks:
  - 1 - mottled blue
  - 2 - yellow wavy stripe
- Baste each foundation in the seam

lowance, halfway between the stitching line and the broken line, to hold the fabrics in place, if desired.

Trim each foundation on the broken line.

Cut the Block B's in half diagonally, as shown.

• Center and stitch half of a Block B to a Block A, as shown.

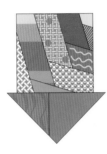

• Stitch a mottled blue triangle to the opposite side of the Block A.

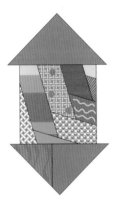

• In the same manner, stitch the second half of the Block B and a mottled blue triangle to the remaining sides of the Block A to complete a Fish block, as shown. Make 6.

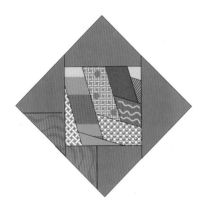

ASSEMBLY

• Lay out 3 Fish blocks in a row, with 2" x 9" mottled blue strips between them. Join the blocks and strips. Make 2.

• Lay out the two rows with the 2" x 29" mottled blue strip between them.

• Join the strip and rows.

• Stitch a 1 1/2" x 25" blue with red dots strip between a 2" x 25" mottled blue strip and a 4" x 25" mottled blue strip, right sides together along their length, to form a short pieced border.

• Stitch a 1 1/2" x 35" blue with red dots strip between a 2" x 35" mottled blue strip and a 4" x 35" mottled blue strip, right sides together along their length, to form a long pieced border.

• In the same manner, make a short and a long pieced border, using the wide stripe strips and the remaining mottled blue strips.

• Beginning at the lower right corner of the quilt, pin the short stripe pieced border to the right edge of the quilt. Stop pinning halfway along the side. NOTE: *The border will be longer than the quilt.*

• Stitch a partial seam, beginning at the edge and stopping halfway across the width of the quilt, as shown.

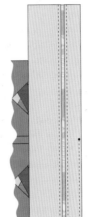

• Stitch the long stripe pieced border to the bottom of the quilt, as shown.

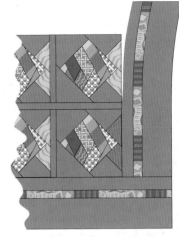

• Stitch the short blue with red dot pieced border to the left side of the quilt and then stitch the long blue with red dot pieced border to the top of the quilt.

• Pin the remainder of the first short border in place and complete the seam.

• Remove the paper foundations now.

• Finish the quilt as described in the *General Directions*, using the 2 1/2" x 44" red with blue dot strips for the binding.

Full-Size Foundation Patterns for Gone Fishin' are on pages 30 and 31

Wading Pool

Splash through this cool quilt with speed-piecing.

Stitch "rippling" cool colors to look like water reflections in **"Wading Pool"** (38" x 44"). Make it in a jiffy with simple cutting and piecing.

QUILT SIZE: 38" x 44"
BLOCK SIZE: 3" square

MATERIALS
Yardage is estimated for 44" fabric.
- 1/4 yard light blue print
- 1/4 yard light green print
- 1/4 yard light wine print
- 1/4 yard light purple print
- 1 1/2 yards dark blue print
- 1/4 yard dark green print
- 1/4 yard dark wine print
- 1/4 yard dark purple print
- 1 1/2 yards backing fabric
- 42" x 48" piece of batting

CUTTING
Dimensions include a 1/4" seam allowance.
- Cut 16: 4 1/4" squares, light blue print
- Cut 16: 4 1/4" squares, light wine print
- Cut 16: 4 1/4" squares, light green print
- Cut 16: 4 1/4" squares, light purple print

- Cut 16: 4 1/4" squares, dark wine print
- Cut 16: 4 1/4" squares, dark green print
- Cut 16: 4 1/4" squares, dark purple print
- Cut 16: 4 1/4" squares, dark blue print
- Cut 2: 2" x 30 1/2" strips, dark blue print
- Cut 2: 2" x 33 1/2" strips, dark blue print
- Cut 4: 2 3/4" x 44" strips, dark blue print
- Cut 4: 2" x 3 1/2" strips, dark blue print
- Cut 5: 2 1/2" x 44" strips, dark blue print, for the binding

PIECING
- Draw diagonal lines from corner to corner, in both directions, on the wrong side of each 4 1/4" light print square, as shown.
- Lay a marked light blue print square

on a 4 1/4" dark blue print square, right sides together, and stitch 1/4" away from one of the drawn lines on both sides, as shown.

- Cut the squares apart on the drawn lines to yield 4 blue pieced triangles.
- Stitch 2 blue pieced triangles together to complete an Hourglass block. Make 28 blue blocks. Set aside the leftover pieced triangles for the corner blocks.

- In the same manner, make 28 wine blocks, setting aside the leftover pieced triangles for the corner blocks.

• In the same manner, make 30 green blocks and 30 purple blocks.

• Lay out 4 blue blocks and 4 purple blocks, alternating colors and block direction, as shown. Stitch them together to complete a blue row. Make 5.

• In the same manner, lay out 4 green blocks and 4 wine blocks, alternating colors and block direction. Stitch them together to complete a green row. Make 5.

• Referring to the quilt photo as needed, lay out the blue rows alternately with the green rows. Join the rows.

• Lay out 3 green blocks, 3 purple blocks, 2 wine blocks and 2 blue blocks, as shown. Join them to form a vertical border. Make 2.

• Stitch a 2" x 30 1/2" dark blue print strip to a long edge of each vertical border, as shown.

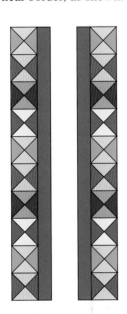

• Referring to the quilt photo as needed, stitch the vertical borders to the long sides of the quilt, keeping the blue print strips against the quilt center.

• Lay out 2 blue blocks, 2 green blocks, 2 purple blocks and 2 wine blocks, as shown. Join them to form a horizontal border. Make 2.

• Stitch a 2" x 3 1/2" dark blue print strip to each short end of the horizontal borders.

• Stitch 2 unmatched left-over pieced triangles together, as shown, to form a corner block. Make 4.

• Stitch a corner block to each end of the horizontal borders, as shown.

• Stitch a 2" x 33 1/2" dark blue print strip to a long edge of each horizontal border, as shown.

• Referring to the quilt photo as needed, stitch the horizontal borders to the remaining sides of the quilt, keeping the dark blue print strips against the quilt center.

• Measure the length of the quilt. Trim two 2 3/4" x 44" dark blue print strips to that measurement and stitch them to the long sides of the quilt.

• Measure the width of the quilt, including the borders. Trim the remaining 2 3/4" x 44" dark blue print strips to that measurement and stitch them to the remaining sides of the quilt.

• Finish the quilt as described in the *General Directions*, using the 2 1/2" x 44" dark blue print strips for the binding.

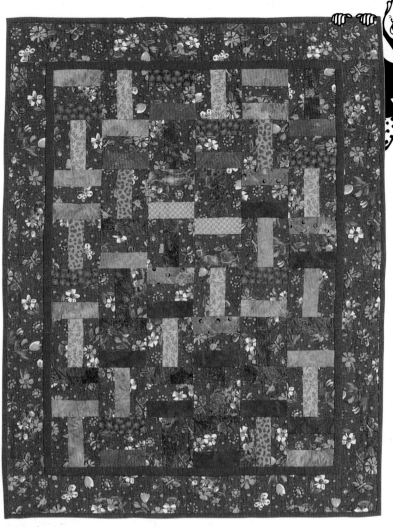

Climbing the Rail Fence

Make a striking quilt with big pieces and easy stitching.

If you're looking for a quickie quilt, **"Climbing the Rail Fence"** (36" x 45") is perfect. I pulled out some of my favorite brights for this project to make sure it would be a small child's delight!

QUILT SIZE: 36" x 45"
BLOCK SIZE: 4 1/2" square

MATERIALS
Yardage is estimated for 44" fabric.
• Assorted bright print scraps in green, blue, orange, fuchsia, red, turquoise, yellow, purple and gold, totaling at least 3/4 yard
• 1 1/4 yards blue print
• 5/8 yard red print
• 1 1/2 yards backing fabric
• 40" x 49" piece of batting

CUTTING
Dimensions include a 1/4" seam allowance.
• Cut 72: 2" x 5" strips, blue print
• Cut 4: 3 3/4" x 42" strips, blue print

• Cut 72: 2" x 5" strips, assorted bright prints
• Cut 4: 1 1/4" x 40" strips, red print
• Cut 5: 2 1/2" x 44" strips, red print, for the binding

PIECING
• Stitch a 2" x 5" bright print strip between two 2" x 5" blue print strips, to form Block A. Make 24.

• Stitch a 2" x 5" blue print strip between

two different 2" x 5" bright print strips, to form Block B. Make 24.

ASSEMBLY
• Lay out 3 Block A's and 3 Block B's, alternating them, as shown. Stitch them together to complete a row. Make 8.

• Referring to the quilt photo as needed,

ay out the 8 rows so that the Block A's and Block B's alternate. Join the rows.

• Measure the length of the quilt. Trim two 1 1/4" x 40" red print strips to that measurement. Stitch them to the long sides of the quilt.

• Measure the width of the quilt, including the borders. Trim the remaining 1 1/4" x 40" red print strips to that measurement. Stitch them to the remaining sides of the quilt.

• In the same manner, trim two 3 3/4" x 42" blue print strips to fit the quilt's length and stitch them to long sides of the quilt.

• Trim the remaining 3 3/4" x 42" blue print strips to fit the quilt's width, and stitch them to the remaining sides of the quilt.

• Finish the quilt as described in the *General Directions*, using the 2 1/2" x 44" red print strips for the binding.

Strip Piecing

If you prefer to strip-piece the blocks, the following directions produce a dozen repeats of 4 identical blocks.

MATERIALS
• 18 bright print strips at least 2" x 22"
• 1 1/4 yards of blue print
• 5/8 yard red print
• 1 1/2 yards backing fabric
• 40" x 49" piece of batting

CUTTING
• Cut 18: 2" x 22" blue print strips
• Cut 18: 2" x 22" assorted bright print strips

PIECING
• Stitch a 2" x 22" bright print strip between two 2" x 22" blue print strips, right sides together along their length. Make 6.
• Cut 5" slices from the pieced strips to yield 24 Block A's.
• Stitch a 2" x 22" blue print strip between two 2" x 22" bright print strips, right sides together along their length. Make 6.
• Cut 5" slices from the pieced strips to yield 24 Block B's.

Little Stars

Frame your little stars with bright colors.

Some of my favorite little people are smiling in this quilt! **"Little Stars"** (37" square) is a cute way to "show off" those that are the closest to your heart.

QUILT SIZE: 37" square
BLOCK SIZE: 10 1/2" square

MATERIALS
Yardage is estimated for 44" fabric.
• 9 color photos transferred to fabric so that the images are at least 4" square NOTE: *When selecting photos for transfer, keep in mind that 1/4" will be lost on each side for the seam allowances.*
• 1/2 yard yellow print
• 1/4 yard second yellow print
• 1/3 yard teal print
• 1/4 yard red print
• 1 yard purple print
• 1/2 yard purple stripe
• 1 1/4 yards backing fabric
• 41" square of batting

CUTTING
Dimensions include a 1/4" seam allowance.
• Cut 9: 4" squares, fabric with photo transfers centered
• Cut 8: 4 3/4" squares, yellow print
• Cut 4: 5 1/4" squares, yellow print
• Cut 4: 4 3/4" squares, second yellow print

• Cut 6: 4 3/4" squares, teal print
• Cut 4: 1 3/4" x 31" strips, teal print
• Cut 6: 4 3/4" squares, purple print
• Cut 16: 2 1/4" squares, purple print
• Cut 4: 5 1/4" squares, purple print
• Cut 4: 4 1/2" x 44" strips, purple print
• Cut 16: 2 1/4" squares, red print
• Cut 4: 1 1/4" x 32" strips, red print
• Cut 4: 2 1/2" x 44" strips, purple stripe, for the binding

PIECING
• Draw diagonal lines from corner to corner on the wrong side of each 5 1/4" yellow print square. Draw horizontal and vertical lines through the centers.
• Place a marked yellow print square on a 5 1/4" purple print square, right sides together. Stitch 1/4" away from the diagonal lines on both sides. Make 4.

• Cut the squares on the drawn lines to yield 32 pieced squares. Press the seam allowances toward the purple print.
• Lay out 2 pieced squares, a 2 1/4" purple print square and a 2 1/4" red print square, as shown.

• Join the squares to form Unit A. Make 16. Set them aside.
• Draw diagonal lines from corner to corner on the wrong side of each 4 3/4" yellow print square.
• Lay a marked 4 3/4" yellow print square on a 4 3/4" purple print square, right sides together, and stitch 1/4" away from one drawn line on both sides, as shown. Make 4.

• Cut the squares apart on the drawn lines to yield 16 purple pieced triangles.
• In the same manner, using marked yellow print squares and 4 3/4" teal print squares, make 16 teal pieced triangles.
• Stitch a teal pieced triangle to a purple

pieced triangle, as shown, to form Unit B. Make 16.

Lay out 4 Unit A's, 4 Unit B's and a 4" photo transfer square, as shown.

Stitch the units into rows and join the rows to complete a block. Make 4.

Draw diagonal lines from corner to corner on the wrong side of each 4 3/4" second yellow print square.

In the same manner as before, using the marked second yellow print squares and the remaining 4 3/4" purple print and teal print squares, make 8 purple pieced triangles and 8 teal pieced triangles.

• Stitch a purple pieced triangle to a teal pieced triangle, as before, to form a pieced sashing unit. Make 8.
• Lay out 4 pieced sashing units and three 4" photo transfer squares, as shown. Join them to form a horizontal sashing.

• Lay out 2 sashing units and a 4" photo transfer square, as shown. Join them to form a vertical sashing. Make 2.

• Stitch a vertical sashing between 2 blocks to form a row, making sure the photos are right side up. Make 2.
• Join the rows with the horizontal sashing between them.
• Measure the length of the quilt. Trim two 1 3/4" x 31" teal print strips to that measurement. Stitch them to the sides of the quilt.
• Measure the width of the quilt, including the borders. Trim the remaining 1 3/4" x 31" teal print strips to that measurement.

Stitch them to the top and bottom of the quilt.
• In the same manner, trim 2 of the 1 1/4" x 32" red print strips to fit the quilt's length and stitch them to the sides of the quilt.
• Trim the remaining 1 1/4" x 32" red print strips to fit the quilt's width, and stitch them to the top and bottom of the quilt.
• Trim 2 of the 4 1/2" x 44" purple print strips to fit the quilt's length and stitch them to the sides of the quilt.
• Trim the remaining 4 1/2" x 44" purple print strips to fit the quilt's width, and stitch them to the top and bottom of the quilt.
• Finish the quilt as described in the *General Directions*, using the 2 1/2" x 44" purple stripe strips for the binding.

Hint

I suggest you place the photo-transfer fabric on top when stitching pieces together. Be careful to only stick pins in the seam allowances of the photo-transfer fabric.

Snail's Trail

Stitch a quilt with lots of visual stimulation.

"Snail's Trail" (38" x 46 1/2") has always been an intriguing design to me. The use of teal, blue and purple in this quilt provides a cool, restful feeling in the midst of a churning pattern.

QUILT SIZE: 38" x 46 1/2"
BLOCK SIZE: 8 1/2" square

MATERIALS

Yardage is estimated for 44" fabric.
- 3/4 yard blue print
- 1/4 yard second blue print
- 1 yard purple print
- 1/2 yard teal print
- 1 1/4 yards light purple print
- 1 1/2 yards backing fabric
- 42" x 51" piece of batting

CUTTING

Dimensions include a 1/4" seam allowance.
- Cut 1: 2" x 44" strip, blue print
- Cut 12: 3 7/8" squares, blue print, then cut them in half diagonally to yield 24 medium triangles
- Cut 4: 2" x 38" strips, blue print
- Cut 4: 2" squares, purple print
- Cut 4: 4 1/4" x 42" strips, purple print

- Cut 5: 2 1/2" x 44" strips, purple print, for the binding
- Cut 4: 5 1/8" squares, second blue print, then cut them in half diagonally to yield 8 large triangles
- Cut 12: 3" squares, teal print, then cut them in half diagonally to yield 24 small triangles
- Cut 8: 5 1/8" squares, teal print, then cut them in half diagonally to yield 16 large triangles
- Cut 1: 2" x 44" strip, light purple print
- Cut 4: 2" squares, light purple print
- Cut 12: 3" squares, light purple print, then cut them in half diagonally to yield 24 small triangles
- Cut 12: 3 7/8" squares, light purple print, then cut them in half diagonally to yield 24 medium triangles
- Cut 12: 5 1/8" squares, light purple print, then cut them in half diagonally to yield 24 large triangles
- Cut 4: 1" x 41" strips, light purple print

PIECING

- Stitch a 2" x 44" blue print strip to a 2" x 44" light purple print strip, along their length.
- Cut twenty 2" slices from the pieced strip, as shown.

- Stitch 2 slices together to form a blue Four-Patch unit. Make 10.

- Stitch a 2" purple print square to a 2" light purple square. Make 4.
- Stitch 2 of the units together to form a

purple Four-Patch unit. Make 2.
- Stitch small teal print triangles to two opposite sides of a Four-Patch unit.

- Stitch small light purple print triangles to the remaining sides of the unit.

- In the same manner, stitch medium blue print triangles to two opposite sides of the unit and light purple print triangles to the remaining sides. Make 12. Set 4 units aside.

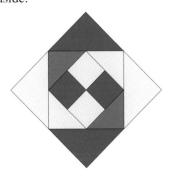

- Stitch large teal print triangles to two opposite sides of a unit, then stitch large light purple print triangles to the remaining sides to complete a block. Make 8.

- Stitch large second blue print triangles to two opposite sides of one of the units you previously set aside. Stitch large light purple print triangles to the remaining sides to complete a block. Make 4.

ASSEMBLY

- Referring to the quilt photo for color placement as desired, lay out the blocks in 4 rows of 3. Stitch the blocks into rows and join the rows.

- Measure the length of the quilt. Trim two 2" x 38" blue print strips to that measurement. Stitch them to the long sides of the quilt.
- Measure the width of the quilt, including the borders. Trim the remaining 2" x 38" blue print strips to that measurement. Stitch them to the remaining sides of the quilt.
- In the same manner, trim 2 of the 1" x 41" light purple print strips to fit the quilt's length and stitch them to the long sides of the quilt.
- Trim the remaining 1" x 41" light purple print strips to fit the quilt's width, and stitch them to the remaining sides of the quilt.
- Trim 2 of the 4 1/4" x 42" purple print strips to fit the quilt's length and stitch them to the long sides of the quilt.
- Trim the remaining 4 1/4" x 42" purple print strips to fit the quilt's width, and stitch them to the remaining sides of the quilt.
- Finish the quilt as described in the *General Directions*, using the 2 1/2" x 44" purple print strips for the binding.

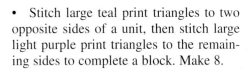

Picture Windows

Create your own adorable view with photos transferred to fabric.

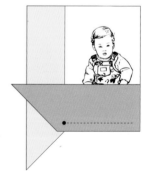

"Picture Windows" (18 1/2" x 22 1/4") displays faces and antics of some of my best friends. It's a wonderful way to frame those you love in a soft setting. This photo quilt would make a thoughtful gift for a special admirer in a child's life.

QUILT SIZE: 18 1/2" x 22 1/4"
BLOCK SIZE: 3 1/2" x 4 3/4"

MATERIALS
Yardage is estimated for 44" fabric.
• 9 color photos transferred to fabric so that the images are at least 3" x 4 1/4" NOTE: *When selecting photos for transfer, keep in mind that 1/4" will be lost on each side for the seam allowances.*
• 1/4 yard red print
• Scrap of second red print, at least 5" square
• 1/4 yard dark green
• Scraps of 2 yellow prints, totaling at least 1/8 yard
• 5/8 yard backing fabric
• 20 1/2" x 24 1/2" piece of batting

CUTTING
Pattern pieces are full size and include a 1/4" seam allowance, as do all dimensions given. Make templates for each of the pattern pieces and cut them out. Reverse the templates and draw around

them on the wrong side of the fabric. Mark the dot.
• Cut 9: 3" x 4 1/4" rectangles, transfer fabric with photos centered
• Cut 7: A, first yellow print
• Cut 2: A, second yellow print
• Cut 6: B, red print
• Cut 4: 2 3/4" x 20" strips, red print
• Cut 3: B, second red print
• Cut 12: 1 1/4" x 5 1/4" strips, dark green
• Cut 4: 1 1/4" x 14" strips, dark green
• Cut 2: 1 3/4" x 44" strips, dark green, for the binding

PIECING
• Stitch a yellow A to the left side of a photo transfer rectangle, stopping and backstitching at the dot, as shown.
• Stitch a red B to the bottom of the photo, keeping the seam allowance of the yel-

low A out of the way. Stop and backstitch at the dot, as before.

• Pin and stitch the remaining seam, from the dot to the edge of the fabric, connecting the yellow A to the red B to complete the block. Make 9.

- Stitch a 1 1/4" x 5 1/4" dark green strip to the right side of each block.
- Stitch 3 blocks together to form a horizontal row. Stitch a 1 1/4" x 5 1/4" dark green strip to the left edge of the row. Make 3.
- Lay out the 3 rows with 1 1/4" x 14" dark green strips between them and at the top and bottom. Join the rows and strips.
- Measure the length of the quilt. Trim two 2 3/4" x 20" red print strips to that measurement. Stitch them to the sides of the quilt.
- Measure the width of the quilt, including the borders. Trim the remaining 2 3/4" x 20" red print strips to that measurement and stitch them to the top and bottom of the quilt.
- Finish the quilt as described in the *General Directions*, using the 1 3/4" x 14" dark green strips for the binding.

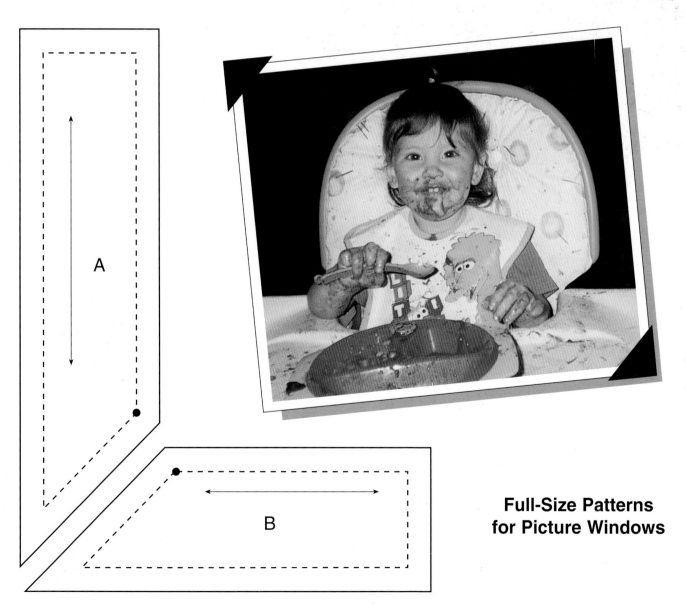

**Full-Size Patterns
for Picture Windows**

Tic-Tac-Toe

A child's board game
and hand-dyed scraps
inspire a modern quilt.

Baby's will love the bright, playful colors in **"Tic-Tac-Toe"** (33" x 36")
I used two simple-to-piece blocks in this imaginary game quilt.

QUILT SIZE: 33" x 36"
BLOCK SIZE: 3 1/4" square

MATERIALS

Yardage is estimated for 44" fabric.
• Assorted hand-dyed scraps, each at least 2 1/2" square
• Assorted print scraps totaling at least 1 3/4 yards
• 3/8 yard hand-dyed blue, for the binding
• 1 1/4 yards backing fabric
• 37" x 40" piece of batting

CUTTING

Dimensions include a 1/4" seam allowance.

For each of 40 Block A's:
• Cut 1: 2 1/4" square, hand-dyed fabric
• Cut 1: 1 1/4" x 2 1/4" strip, print or hand-dyed fabric
• Cut 2: 1 1/4" x 3" strips, print or hand-dyed fabric
• Cut 1: 1 1/4" x 3 3/4" strip, print or hand-dyed fabric

For each of 41 Block B's:
• Cut 1: 2" square, hand-dyed fabric
• Cut 2: 3 1/8" squares, print or hand-dyed fabric, then cut them in half diagonally to yield 4 triangles

Also:
• Cut 9: 1 1/4" x 10 1/4" strips, assorted prints or hand-dyed fabrics
• Cut 22: 1 1/4" x 11" strips, assorted prints or hand-dyed fabrics
• Cut 5: 1 1/4" x 11 3/4" strips, assorted prints or hand-dyed fabrics
• Cut 4: 2 1/2" x 44" strips, hand-dyed blue, for the binding

PIECING

For the Block A's:
• Stitch a 1 1/4" x 2 1/4" print or hand-dyed strip to one side of a 2 1/4" hand-dyed square, as shown.

• Stitch a 1 1/4" x 3" print or hand-dyed strip to an adjacent side of the square, as shown.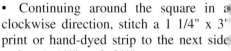
• Continuing around the square in a clockwise direction, stitch a 1 1/4" x 3" print or hand-dyed strip to the next side and a 1 1/4" x 3 3/4" print or hand-dyed strip to the last side to complete a Block A. Make 40. Set them aside.

For the Block B's:
• Stitch matching print or hand-dyed triangles to opposite sides of a 2" hand-dyed square, as shown. Press the seam allowance toward the square.

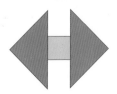

Overlapping the triangles, stitch same print triangles to the remaining sides of the square. Trim the excess fabric from the back, leaving a 1/4" seam allowance, to complete Block B. Make 41.

ASSEMBLY

• Lay out 4 Block A's and 5 Block B's in 3 rows of 3, as shown.
• Join the blocks to complete a Unit 1, as shown. Make 5.

Unit 1

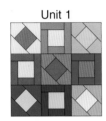

• Lay out 5 Block A's and 4 Block B's, as shown, and join them to complete a Unit 2. Make 4.

Unit 2

• Stitch a 1 1/4" x 10 1/4" print strip to the bottom of each unit, as shown.

 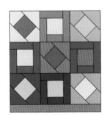

• Stitch a 1 1/4" x 11" print strip to the left side of each unit, as shown.

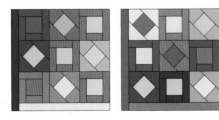

• Stitch two 1 1/4" x 11" print strips and one 1 1/4" x 11 3/4" print strip together,

end to end as shown, to form an outer sashing. Make 4.

| 11" | 11" | 11 3/4" |

• Referring to the Assembly Diagram, lay out 3 rows of 3 blocks. Place sashings between the rows and at the top and bottom of the quilt, keeping the 11 3/4" strips toward the right side.
• Stitch a 1 1/4" x 11" print strip to the top of each of the first 3 blocks.
• Stitch the blocks into horizontal rows.
• Stitch a 1 1/4" x 11 3/4" print strip to the end of the first row.
• Stitch a 1 1/4" x 11" strip to the end of each remaining row.
• Join the rows and sashings.
• Finish the quilt as described in the *General Directions*, using the 2 1/2" x 44" hand-dyed blue strips for the binding.

Assembly Diagram

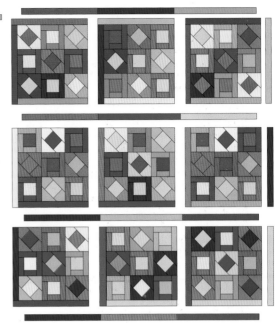

Alphabet Quilt

Appliqué
the ABC's
on this
unique design.

Sharyn Craig of El Cajon, California, stitched this adorable **"Alphabet Quilt"** (42 1/2" x 48 1/2") with bright primary colors. Sharyn made this quilt for her first grandbaby.

QUILT SIZE: 42 1/2" x 48 1/2"
BLOCK SIZE: 4 1/4" square

MATERIALS
Yardage is estimated for 44" fabric.
- Assorted bright prints in red, green, blue and yellow, totaling at least 3/4 yard
- 1 yard white print
- 1/2 yard red print, for the first border
- 3/8 yard yellow print, for the second border
- 3/4 yard blue star print for the third border
- 2 3/4 yards backing fabric
- 47" x 53" piece of batting
- Fusible web

CUTTING
Appliqué patterns (on pages 22 and 23) are full size and do not need a seam allowance. Reverse the patterns and trace around them on the paper side of the fusible web. Cut them out slightly beyond the traced line. Fuse them to the wrong side of the appropriate color scrap and cut them out on the line. All other dimensions include a 1/4" seam allowance.
- Cut 10: 3" squares, bright red prints, in matching pairs
- Cut 15: 2 5/8" squares, bright red prints, then cut 5 of them in half diagonally to yield 10 triangles
- Cut 10: 3" squares, bright green prints, in matching pairs
- Cut 14: 2 5/8" squares, bright green prints, then cut 6 of them in half diagonally to yield 12 triangles
- Cut 6: 3" squares, bright yellow prints, in matching pairs
- Cut 7: 2 5/8" squares, bright yellow prints, then cut 5 of them in half diagonally to yield 10 triangles
- Cut 14: 3" squares, bright blue prints, in matching pairs
- Cut 20: 2 5/8" squares, bright blue prints, then cut 8 of them in half diagonally to yield 16 triangles
- Cut 40: 3" squares, white print
- Cut 12: 3 1/2" squares, white print
- Cut 18: 2 5/8" squares, white print
- Cut 18: 4 3/4" squares, white print
- Cut 9: 4 1/4" squares, red border print then cut them in quarters diagonally to yield 36 small triangles
- Cut 2: 4" squares, red border print then cut them in half diagonally to yield 4 large triangles
- Cut 4: 2 1/2" x 44" strips, red border print
- Cut 4: 1 1/2" x 44" strips, yellow border print
- Cut 4: 3 1/2" x 44" strips, blue star print
- Cut 5: 2 1/2" x 44" strips, blue star print, for the binding

PREPARATION
- Draw a diagonal line from corner to corner on the wrong side of each 3" white

print square and each 2 5/8" bright print square.

PIECING

• Lay a marked 3" white print square on a 3" red print square, right sides together, and sew 1/4" away from the diagonal line on both sides. Cut on the marked line to yield 2 pieced squares. Repeat, using a matching red print square.

• Lay out the 4 pieced squares, as shown. Join them to complete a Pinwheel block. NOTE: *Make sure all your pinwheel blocks spin in the same direction.*

• Make 5 red, 5 green, 7 blue and 3 yellow Pinwheel blocks. NOTE: *Because of the interlocking nature of the design, it is best to lay out all of the remaining pieces of the quilt before sewing additional blocks.*

• On a design wall or other flat surface at least 32" x 38", and referring to the quilt photo for color placement, lay out the pinwheels, on point, in 5 rows of 4.

• Lay 3 1/2" white print squares between the blocks, as shown.

• Lay a coordinating print triangle along each edge of the white print squares, making sure that each triangle forms a same-color diamond shape with the bright print adjacent pinwheel triangle.

• Remove the first white print square and 4 adjacent print triangles from the layout. Center and stitch 2 of the triangles to opposite sides of the white square, as shown, keeping them in the proper order.

• Center and stitch the remaining trian-

gles to the remaining sides of the square to complete a Square-in-a-Square block. Return it to the lay-out, making sure to place it in the correct direction, so that the colors match the adjacent Pinwheel blocks.

• Stitch the remaining Square-in-a-Square blocks in the same manner.

• Referring to the Assembly Diagram as needed, stitch the blocks into diagonal rows, but do not join the rows yet. Return the rows to the layout.

• Lay a 4 3/4" white print square at the end of each diagonal row.

• Paying attention to color placement, place a marked 2 5/8" bright print square right side down wherever a triangle is needed to complete the outer points of the Pinwheel blocks, as shown.

• Remove the 4 3/4" white print square and the 2 5/8" red print square from the upper left corner of the lay-out. Stitch on the marked line.

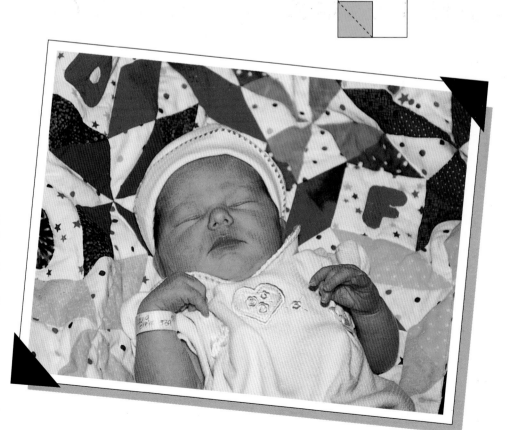

- Trim 1/4" beyond the seam. Open the unit and press the seam allowance toward the red print. Return the unit to the layout, making sure the red triangle touches the red triangle in the Pinwheel block.
- In the same manner, remove the pieces for the next end block from the layout. Stitch the first print square and trim as before.
- Lay the second marked print square on the adjacent corner of the white print square, making sure it is in the correct location to complete the outer star points of the Pinwheel block. Stitch and trim as before, and return the end block to the layout.

- Stitch the remaining end blocks in the same manner. Stitch them to the ends of the diagonal rows.
- Stitch small red print triangles to adjacent sides of a 2 5/8" white print square to complete a triangle unit. Make 18.

- Referring to the quilt photo, lay out the triangle units along the edges of the quilt. Lay a large red print triangle in each corner.
- Stitch the triangle units and large red print triangles to the diagonal rows and join the rows.
- Measure the length of the quilt. Trim two 2 1/2" x 44" red print strips to that measurement and stitch them to the long sides of the quilt.
- Measure the width of the quilt, including the borders. Trim the remaining 2 1/2 x 44" red print strips to that measurement and stitch them to the remaining sides of

Full-Size Appliqué Patterns for Alphabet Quilt

the quilt.
• In the same manner, trim 2 of the 1 1/2" x 44" yellow print strips to fit the quilt's length and stitch them to the long sides of the quilt.
• Trim the remaining 1 1/2" x 44" yellow print strips to fit the quilt's width, including the borders, and stitch them to

the remaining sides of the quilt.
• Trim 2 of the 3 1/2" x 44" blue print strips to fit the quilt's length and stitch them to the long sides of the quilt.
• Trim the remaining 3 1/2" x 44" blue print strips to fit the quilt's width, including the borders, and stitch them to the remaining sides of the quilt.

• Referring to the quilt photo as needed, fuse the appliqué alphabet pieces in place, following the manufacturer's directions.
• Stitch around the alphabet pieces with a machine zigzag or buttonhole stitch.
• Finish the quilt as described in the *General Directions*, using the 2 1/2" x 44" blue print strips for the binding.

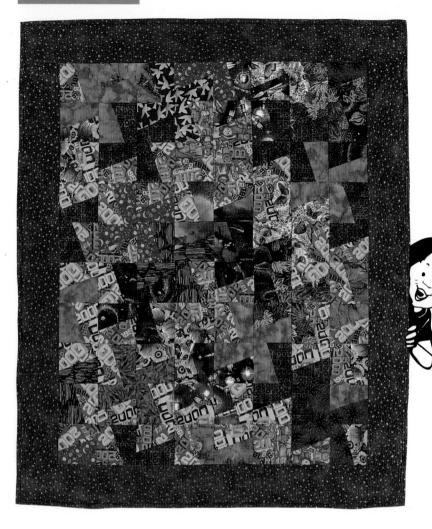

Pinwheels in the Wind

Who says one-patch designs are quiet and monotonous? Not me!

"Pinwheels in the Wind" (40 1/2" x 48 1/2") uses brightly colored millennium fabric. I encourage you to do the same. Fabric with the year 2000 printed on it is especially appropriate for birthday quilts made during this momentous year.

QUILT SIZE: 40 1/2" x 48 1/2"
BLOCK SIZE: 8" square

MATERIALS
Yardage is estimated for 44" fabric.
- Assorted bright prints, totaling at least 1 3/4 yards
- 1 yard blue print
- 1 1/2 yards backing fabric
- 44" x 53" piece of batting

CUTTING
Dimensions include a 1/4" seam allowance.
For each of 20 pinwheels:
- Cut 4: A, bright print
- Cut 4: A, contrasting bright print
Also:
- Cut 4: 4 1/2" x 44" strips, blue print
- Cut 5: 2 1/2" x 44" strips, blue print, for the binding

PIECING
- To achieve the interlocking design, it is best to lay out all of the pieces for the quilt

before stitching the blocks. NOTE: *A Coloring Diagram is provided on the facing page for those of you who prefer to plan color placement using this method.*
- On a design wall or other flat surface at least 36" x 46", lay out 4 matching A's to form a pinwheel, as shown.

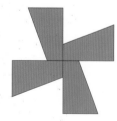

- Continue laying out pinwheels in 5 rows of 4, as shown in the Assembly Diagram.
- Lay contrasting A's in the spaces between the original A's. Refer to the quilt photo as needed so that the contrasting A's form interlocking pinwheels between the original pinwheels and along the edges of the quilt.
- Beginning in the upper left corner,

stitch each pair of A's together along the bias edge, as shown, to form a pieced unit.

- After sewing each unit, return it to the lay-out, making sure the units remain in order and are turned in the correct direction.
- Stitch the units into rows and join the rows.
- Measure the length of the quilt. Trim two 4 1/2" x 44" blue print strips to that measurement and stitch them to the long sides of the quilt.
- Measure the width of the quilt, including the borders. Trim the remaining 4 1/2" x 44" blue print strips to that measurement and stitch them to the remaining sides of the quilt.
- Finish the quilt as described in the *General Directions*, using the 2 1/2" x 44" blue print strips for the binding.

Assembly Diagram

Coloring Diagram for Pinwheels in the Wind

Full-Size Pattern for Pinwheels in the Wind

A

Baby's First Nine-Patch

Here's a favorite block made new with a colorful setting!

When Stacey, Chitra Publications staff member, announced she was expecting, the rest of the staff started making plans for a baby quilt. Each employee was given a stack of 2" squares and told to make Nine-Patch blocks. Debra Feece assembled the quilt and Elsie Campbell quilted **"Baby's First Nine Patch"** (47" square) for new little Caleigh Rae.

QUILT SIZE: 47" square
BLOCK SIZE: 4 1/2" square

MATERIALS
Yardage is estimated for 44" fabric.
• Assorted print scraps, each at least 2" square
• 1/4 yard white
• 3/8 yard yellow
• 1/2 yard pale green
• 1 yard green stripe
• 1/2 yard green print
• 3 yards backing fabric
• 51" square of batting

CUTTING
Dimensions include a 1/4" seam allowance.
• Cut 441: 2" squares, assorted prints
• Cut 4: 5" squares, white
• Cut 12: 5" squares, yellow

• Cut 20: 5" squares, pale green
• Cut 12: 6 1/4" squares, green stripe, then cut them in half diagonally to yield 24 setting triangles. NOTE: *Cut these squares on the bias, with the stripe running diagonally from corner to corner if you wish to achieve the same look as in the quilt. These pieces must be handled carefully when stitching, pressing and quilting to avoid stretching. Alternatively, if you substitute a non-directional fabric for the border, you may cut the squares on the straight grain and cut 6: 9 1/4" squares, then cut them in quarters diagonally to yield 24 setting triangles.*
• Cut 2: 6 1/4" squares, green stripe, then cut them in half diagonally to yield 4 corner triangles. NOTE: *Cut these squares on the bias if your fabric is striped, but on the straight grain if you substitute a non-directional border fabric.*

• Cut 5: 2 1/2" x 44" strips, green print, for the binding

PIECING
• Lay out nine 2" assorted print squares. Stitch the squares into rows and join the rows to complete a Nine-Patch Block, as shown. Make 49.

• Lay out 7 rows of 7 blocks on point.
• Referring to the quilt photo for color placement, lay out the white, yellow and pale green squares between the pieced blocks.

- Referring to the Assembly Diagram, add the green stripe corner and setting triangles along the outside edges.
- Stitch the blocks together in diagonal rows and join the rows. NOTE: *The green stripe triangles will overlap to form a border.*
- After stitching the rows together, trim the excess fabric from the back of the overlap, leaving a 1/4" seam allowance. Trim to square the corners even with the sides of the quilt.
- Finish the quilt as described in the *General Directions*, using the 2 1/2" x 44" green print strips for the binding.

Assembly Diagram

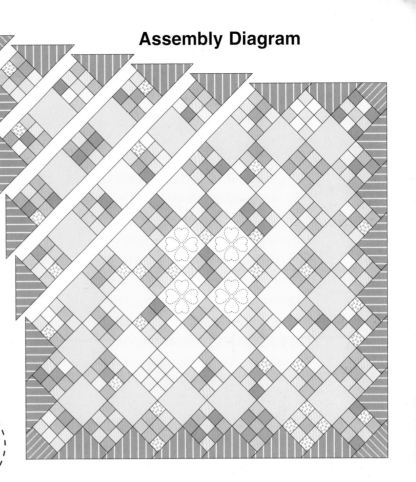

Full-Size Quilting Design

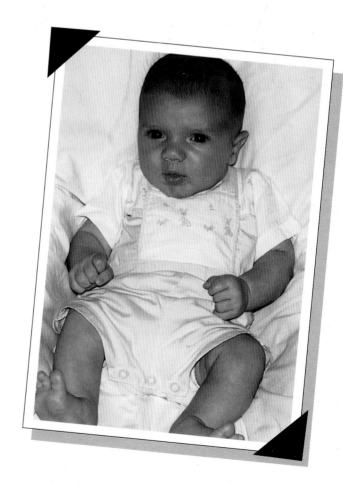

Four-Patch Confetti

Make this bright, bold quilt in a weekend!

Babies love bright colors so that's exactly what I used in **"Four-Patch Confetti"** (40" x 49"). I can envision this quilt as a young child's treasured favorite.

QUILT SIZE: 40" x 49"
BLOCK SIZE: 3" square

MATERIALS
Yardage is estimated for 44" fabric.
- 3/4 yard white-on-white print
- Assorted bright prints, totaling 1 yard
- 1/3 yard purple print
- 1 1/8 yards red print
- 1 1/2 yards backing fabric
- 44" x 53" piece of batting

CUTTING
Dimensions include a 1/4" seam allowance.
- Cut 54: 3 1/2" squares, white-on-white print
- Cut 4: 1 1/4" x 44" strips, white-on-white print
- Cut 24: 2" x 22" strips, assorted bright prints
- Cut 4: 2" x 40" strips, purple print
- Cut 4: 4 1/2" x 44" strips, red print
- Cut 5: 2 1/2" x 44" strips, red print, for the binding

DIRECTIONS
- Stitch two 2" x 22" contrasting print strips together, along their length. Make 12.
- Cut ten 2" slices from each pieced strip, as shown.

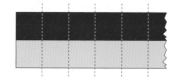

- Join 2 matching slices to complete a Four-Patch block. Make 54. You will have 12 slices left over.

- Referring to the quilt photo as needed, lay out the Four-Patch blocks and the 3 1/2" white-on-white squares in 12 rows of 9, alternating blocks and squares.
- Stitch the blocks into rows and join the rows.
- Measure the length of the quilt. Trim two 2" x 40" purple print strips to that measurement. Stitch them to the long sides of the quilt.

Measure the width of the quilt, including the borders. Trim the remaining 2" x 40" purple print strips to that measurement. Stitch them to the remaining sides of the quilt.

In the same manner, trim 2 of the 1 1/4" x 44" white-on-white print strips to fit the quilt's length and stitch them to the long sides of the quilt.

• Trim the remaining 1 1/4" x 44" white-on-white print strips to fit the quilt's width and stitch them to the remaining sides of the quilt.

• Trim 2 of the 4 1/2" x 44" red print strips to fit the quilt's length and stitch them to the long sides of the quilt.

• Trim the remaining 4 1/2" x 44" red print strips to fit the quilt's width and stitch them to the remaining sides of the quilt.

• Finish the quilt as described in the *General Directions*, using the 2 1/2" x 44" red print strips for the binding.

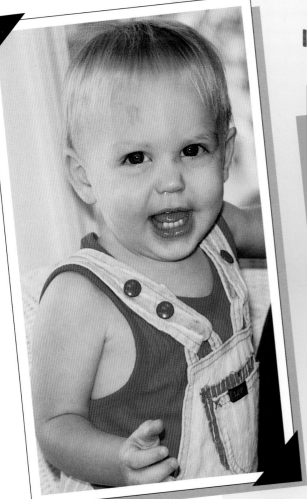

I'd like to thank the following individuals for the contributions they've made to this book:

The children whose photos enliven the pages:

Ambrose • Ashlyn • Bruce
Caleigh Rae • Charles • Colvin
Daniel • Diane • Evan • Jessica
Jonathan • Kasondra • Keanyn
MacKenzie • Maxwell • Morgan
Nathan • Reece • Sara

The parents who, through these photos, have allowed us a glimpse into the wonder that is childhood

Joanie Keith, whose skillful machine quilting adds delight and dimension to my quilts

Finally, my appreciation to the following companies for providing fabric which appears in some of the quilts:

P&B Textiles • Alexander Henry
South Sea Imports • Starr Designs
Alaska Dyeworks

General Directions

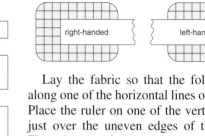

About The Patterns

Read through all directions. Template patterns are full size and, unless otherwise noted, include a 1/4" seam allowance. The solid line is the cutting line; the dashed line is the stitching line. Yardage requirements are based on 44"-wide fabric. Pattern directions are given in step-by-step order.

Fabrics

I suggest using 100% cotton. Wash fabric in warm water with mild detergent and no fabric softener. Wash darks separately and check for bleeding during the rinse cycle. If the color needs to be set, mix equal parts of white vinegar and table salt with water and soak the fabric in it. Dry fabric on a warm-to-hot setting to shrink it. Press it with a hot dry iron to remove any wrinkles.

Rotary Cutting

Begin by folding the fabric in half, selvage to selvage. Make sure the selvages are even and the fold edge is smooth. Fold the fabric in half again, bringing the fold and the selvages together, again making sure everything is smooth and flat.

Position the folded fabric on a cutting mat so that the fabric extends to the right for right-handed people, or to the left for left-handed people. (Mats with grid lines are recommended because the lines serve as guides to help ensure that cut strips will be straight.)

Lay the fabric so that the fold edge is along one of the horizontal lines on the mat. Place the ruler on one of the vertical lines just over the uneven edges of the fabric. The ruler must be absolutely perpendicular to the folded edge. Trim the uneven edge with a rotary cutter. Hold the rotary cutter at a 45° angle to the mat. Make a clean cut through the fabric, beginning in front of the folds and cutting through to the opposite edge with one clean (not short and choppy)

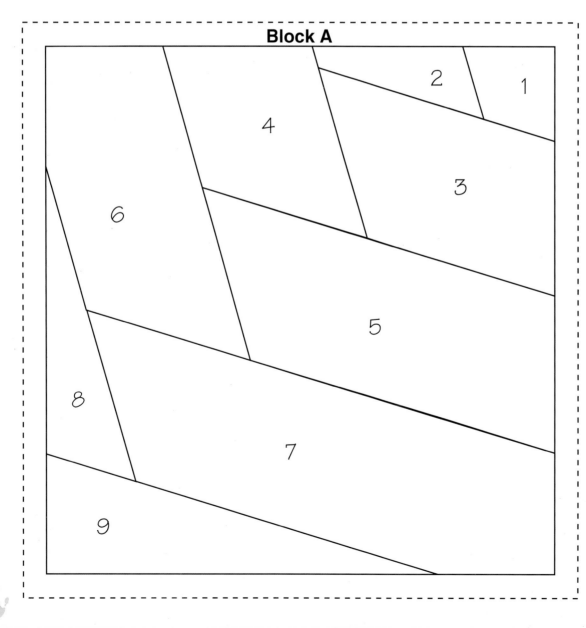

Block A

1 2 3 4 5 6 7 8 9

Full-Size Foundation Pattern for Gone Fishin'